©2019, Cut It Out Publishers. All rights reserved. No part of this publication may be reproduced or distributed in any form or by any means, or stored in any database or retrieval system, without the prior written permission of the publisher.

ISBN: 978-0-578-45049-0

Published by Cut It Out Publishers
Sleepy Hollow, New York 10591
http://thesederbook.com

Who Knows One?
Sing or take turns reading each question and answer.

Who knows one? I know one.
One is our God in Heaven and Earth

Who knows two? I know two.
Two are the tablets of the covenant
One is our God in Heaven and Earth

Who knows three. I know three.
Three are the patriarchs
Two are the tablets of the covenant
One is our God in Heaven and Earth

Who knows four? I know four.
Four are the matriarchs
Three are the patriarchs
Two are the tablets of the covenant
One is our God in Heaven and Earth

Who knows five? I know five.
Five are the books of the Torah
Four are the matriarchs
Three are the patriarchs
Two are the tablets of the covenant
One is our God in Heaven and Earth

Who knows six? I know six.
Six are the orders of the Mishnah
Five are the books of the Torah
Four are the matriarchs
Three are the patriarchs
Two are the tablets of the covenant
One is our God in Heaven and Earth

Who knows seven? I know seven.
Seven are the days of the week
Six are the orders of the Mishnah
Five are the books of the Torah
Four are the matriarchs
Three are the patriarchs
Two are the tablets of the covenant
One is our God in Heaven and Earth

Who knows eight? I know eight.
Eight are the days for circumcision
Seven are the days of the week
Six are the orders of the Mishnah
Five are the books of the Torah
Four are the matriarchs
Three are the patriarchs
Two are the tablets of the covenant
One is our God in Heaven and Earth

Who knows nine? I know nine.
Nine are the months of childbirth
Eight are the days for circumcision
Seven are the days of the week
Six are the orders of the Mishnah
Five are the books of the Torah
Four are the matriarchs
Three are the patriarchs
Two are the tablets of the covenant
One is our God in Heaven and Earth

Who knows ten? I know ten.
Ten are the Words from Sinai
Nine are the months of childbirth
Eight are the days for circumcision
Seven are the days of the week
Six are the orders of the Mishnah
Five are the books of the Torah
Four are the matriarchs
Three are the patriarchs
Two are the tablets of the covenant
One is our God in Heaven and Earth

Who knows eleven? I know eleven.
Eleven are the stars
Ten are the Words from Sinai
Nine are the months of childbirth
Eight are the days for circumcision
Seven are the days of the week
Six are the orders of the Mishnah
Five are the books of the Torah
Four are the matriarchs
Three are the patriarchs
Two are the tablets of the covenant
One is our God in Heaven and Earth

Who knows twelve? I know twelve!
Twelve are the tribes
Eleven are the stars
Ten are the Words from Sinai
Nine are the months of childbirth
Eight are the days for circumcision
Seven are the days of the week
Six are the orders of the Mishnah
Five are the books of the Torah
Four are the matriarchs
Three are the patriarchs
Two are the tablets of the covenant
One is our God in Heaven and Earth

Who knows thirteen? I know thirteen
Thirteen are the attributes of God
Twelve are the tribes
Eleven are the stars
Ten are the Words from Sinai
Nine are the months of childbirth
Eight are the days for circumcision
Seven are the days of the week
Six are the orders of the Mishnah
Five are the books of the Torah
Four are the matriarchs
Three are the patriarchs
Two are the tablets of the covenant
One is our God in Heaven and Earth

Chad Gadya

Sing or recite.

Chad gadya, chad gadya
Dizabin abah bitrei zuzei
Chad gadya, chad gadya.

One little goat, one little goat:
That my father brought for two zuzim.

One little goat, one little goat:
The cat came and ate the goat,
That my father bought for two zuzim.

One little goat, one little goat:
The dog came and bit the cat
That ate the goat,
that my father bought for two zuzim.

One little goat, one little goat:
The stick came and beat the dog
That bit the cat that ate the goat,
That my father bought for two zuzim.

One little goat, one little goat:
The fire came and burned the stick
That beat the dog that bit the cat
That ate the goat,
That my father bought for two zuzim.

One little goat, one little goat:
The water came and extinguished the
Fire that burned the stick
That beat the dog that bit the cat
That ate the goat,
That my father bought for two zuzim.

One little goat, one little goat:
The ox came and drank the water
That extinguished the fire
That burned the stick that beat the dog
That bit the cat that ate the goat,
That my father bought for two zuzim.

One little goat, one little goat:
The butcher came and killed the ox,
That drank the water
That extinguished the fire
That burned the stick that beat the dog
That bit the cat that ate the goat,
That my father bought for two zuzim.

One little goat, one little goat:
The angle of death came and slew
The butcher who killed the ox,
That drank the water
That extinguished the fire
That burned the stick that beat the dog
That bit the cat that ate the goat,
That my father bought for two zuzim.

One little goat, one little goat:
The Holy One, Blessed Be He came and
Smote the angle of death who slew
The butcher who killed the ox,
That drank the water
That extinguished the fire
That burned the stick that beat the dog
That bit the cat that ate the goat,
That my father bought for two zuzim.

Psalm 114 - Hallel

When Israel came forth out of Egypt, the house of Jacob from a people of strange language;
Judah became His sanctuary, Israel His dominion.
The sea saw it, and fled; the Jordan turned backward.
The mountains skipped like rams, the hills like young sheep.
What aileth thee, O thou sea, that thou fleest? thou Jordan, that thou turnest backward?
Ye mountains, that ye skip like rams; ye hills, like young sheep?
Tremble, thou earth, at the presence of the Lord, at the presence of the God of Jacob;
Who turned the rock into a pool of water, the flint into a fountain of waters.
O Israel, trust thou in the LORD! He is their help and their shield!
O house of Aaron, trust ye in the LORD! He is their help and their shield!
Ye that fear the LORD, trust in the LORD! He is their help and their shield.

Step 14: Nirtzah—Acceptance

After reciting the Hallel, recite the blessing over wine again and drink the fourth cup, reclining.

בָּרוּךְ אַתָּה יְיָ, אֱלֹהֵינוּ מֶלֶךְ הָעוֹלָם, בּוֹרֵא פְּרִי הַגָּפֶן:

Bo-ruch a-toh Ado-noi E-lo-hei-nu me-lech ho-olom, bor-ei p'ree ha-ga-fen.

We praise God, Ruler of Everything, who creates the fruit of the vine.

Our Seder is over. We are happy to be here together and we hope to gather to do the same in the years to come. We pray that God brings health and healing to all the people of the world, especially those impacted by natural tragedy and war. Let us say:

לְשָׁנָה הַבָּאָה בִּירוּשָׁלָיִם:

L'shana haba-ah biy'rush-a-la-yim

NEXT YEAR IN JERUSALEM!

אֵלִיָּהוּ הַנָּבִיא, אֵלִיָּהוּ הַתִּשְׁבִּי,
אֵלִיָּהוּ, אֵלִיָּהוּ,אֵלִיָּהוּ הַגִּלְעָדִי.
בִּמְהֵרָה בְיָמֵנוּ יָבוֹא אֵלֵינוּ
עִם מָשִׁיחַ בֶּן דָּוִד,
עִם מָשִׁיחַ בֶּן דָּוִד.

Eliyahu hanavi
Eliyahu hatishbi
Eliyahu, Eliyahu, Eliyahu hagiladi
Bimheirah b'yameinu, yavo eileinu
Im mashiach ben-David,
Im mashiach ben-David

**Elijah the prophet, the returning,
the man of Gilad:
return to us speedily, in our days with the
messiah, son of David.**

The Cup of Elijah

Refill the wine glasses one last time. Now fill Elijah's cup and open the front door to invite the prophet to join our Seder.

One way to fill Elijah's cup of wine is for all participants to pour a little of their own wine into the prophet's cup, symbolizing our responsibility to bring about redemption.

Step 12: Berach—Blessings After the Meal

Jewish meals always conclude with a blessing, and so does this meal. While the meal is over, the Seder is not.

Pour the third cup of wine in each glass and recite the following Grace:

We praise God, Ruler of Everything, whose goodness sustains the world.
You are the origin of love and compassion, the source of bread for all.
Thanks to You, we need never lack for food; You provide food enough for everyone.
We praise God, source of food for everyone.
As it says in the Torah: When you have eaten and are satisfied,
give praise to your God who has given you this good earth.
We praise God for the earth and for its sustenance.
Renew our spiritual center in our time. We praise God, who centers us.
May the source of peace grant peace to us, to the Jewish people, and to the entire world.
Amen.

Bless the wine:

בָּרוּךְ אַתָּה יְיָ, אֱלֹהֵינוּ מֶלֶךְ הָעוֹלָם, בּוֹרֵא פְּרִי הַגָּפֶן:

Bo-ruch a-toh Ado-noi E-lo-hei-nu me-lech ho-olom, bor-ei p'ree ha-ga-fen.

We praise God, Ruler of Everything, who creates the fruit of the vine.

Drink the third glass of wine!

Step 11: Tzafun—Out of Hiding

The last food that is officially eaten at the Seder is a piece of the afikomen matzah. If the children have hidden or stolen the afikomen, they must return it now because the Seder cannot be concluded without it.

The Seder represents the journey from enslavement to freedom. The afikomen symbolizes the Pesach Sacrifice eaten at the end of the meal. The afikomen also represents the part of the self or soul that is lost or given up in enslavement. Tzafun represents our reclaiming the pieces of self that were missing. We ingest these symbols to internalize their meaning.

After eating the afikoman, we do not eat or drink anything except for the two remaining cups of wine.

Step 10: Shulchan Orech—the Meal

It's time for the Seder meal. Let's eat!

Step 9: Korech—the Sandwich

> Two thousand years ago, Hillel combined matzah, a slice of the Paschal Lamb, and a bitter herb. Jews no longer sacrifice a lamb, so the Passover sandwich is only matzah, charoset, and a bitter herb.

While we do not make sacrifices any more, we honor this custom by eating a sandwich of the remaining matzah and bitter herbs. Some people will also include charoset in the sandwich to remind us that God's kindness helped relieve the bitterness of slavery.

Break off two pieces of the bottom matzah. Place bitter herbs dipped in the charoset between the two pieces of matzah. Recite the blessing and eat the sandwich while reclining.

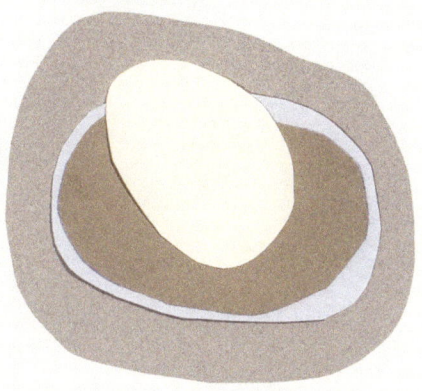

> Eggs represent the circle of life

26

Step 8: Maror—the Bitter Herbs

Dip the bitter herbs in the charoset. No reclining this time!

In creating a holiday about the joy of freedom, we turn the story of our bitter history into a sweet celebration. We symbolize this by dipping our bitter herbs into the sweet charoset. We don't totally eradicate the taste of the bitter with the taste of the sweet… but, doesn't the sweet mean more when it's layered over the bitterness?

בָּרוּךְ אַתָּה יְיָ אֱלֹהֵינוּ מֶלֶךְ הָעוֹלָם, אֲשֶׁר קִדְּשָׁנוּ בְּמִצְוֹתָיו וְצִוָּנוּ עַל אֲכִילַת מָרוֹר:

Bo-ruch a-toh Ado-noi E-lo-hei-nu me-lech ho-olom, asher kid'shanu b'mitzvotav v'tzivanu al achilat maror.

We praise God, Ruler of Everything, who made us holy through obligations, commanding us to eat bitter herbs.

The bitter herbs remind us of the bitterness of slavery.

Step 7: Motzi Matzah—We Eat the Matzah

Take hold of the three matzah (the broken one between the two whole ones) and recite the customary blessing before bread.

בָּרוּךְ אַתָּה יְיָ, אֱלֹהֵינוּ מֶלֶךְ הָעוֹלָם, הַמּוֹצִיא לֶחֶם מִן הָאָרֶץ:

Bo-ruch a-toh Ado-noi E-lo-hei-nu me-lech ho-olom, ha-motzi lechem min ha-aretz.

We praise God, Ruler of Everything, who brings bread from the land.

Place the bottom matzah back onto the plate, and hold the top whole matzah with the broken middle one and recite:

בָּרוּךְ אַתָּה יְיָ, אֱלֹהֵינוּ מֶלֶךְ הָעוֹלָם, אֲשֶׁר קִדְּשָׁנוּ בְּמִצְוֹתָיו וְצִוָּנוּ עַל אֲכִילַת מַצָּה:

Bo-ruch a-toh Ado-noi E-lo-hei-nu me-lech ho-olom, asher kid'shanu b'mitzvotav v'tzivanu al achilat matzah.

We praise God, Ruler of Everything, who made us holy through obligations, commanding us to eat matzah.

Distribute the top and middle matzah for everyone to eat.

The Second Glass of Wine

We praise God, Ruler of Everything, who redeemed us and our ancestors from slavery, enabling us to reach this night and eat matzah and bitter herbs. May we continue to reach future holidays in peace and happiness.

בָּרוּךְ אַתָּה יְיָ, אֱלֹהֵינוּ מֶלֶךְ הָעוֹלָם, בּוֹרֵא פְּרִי הַגָּפֶן:

Bo-ruch a-toh Ado-noi E-lo-hei-nu me-lech ho-olom, borei p'ree hagafen.

We praise God, Ruler of Everything, who creates the fruit of the vine.

The child's questioning triggers one of the most significant mitzvot of Passover, which is the highlight of the Seder ceremony: the Haggadah, telling the story of the Exodus from Egypt.

Drink the second glass of wine!

Step 6: Rochtzah—Washing Before the Meal

The hands are washed again, this time with the customary blessings usually done before eating bread.

בָּרוּךְ אַתָּה יְיָ אֱלֹהֵינוּ מֶלֶךְ הָעוֹלָם, אֲשֶׁר קִדְּשָׁנוּ בְּמִצְוֹתָיו, וְצִוָּנוּ עַל נְטִילַת יָדָיִם:

Bo-ruch a-toh Ado-noi E-lo-hei-nu me-lech ho-olom, asher kid-shanu b'mitz-vo-tav v'tzi-vanu al n'tilat ya-da-yim.

We praise God, Ruler of Everything, who made us holy through obligations, commanding us to wash our hands.

It's customary not to speak at all between washing your hands and saying the blessings over the matzah. You can use this time to reflect on the sanctification and purification that you're undergoing.

The Passover Symbols

Rabban Gamliel says that whoever doesn't explain the shank bone, matzah, and marror (or bitter herbs) hasn't done Passover justice.

בְּכָל־דּוֹר וָדוֹר חַיָּב אָדָם לִרְאוֹת אֶת־עַצְמוֹ, כְּאִלּוּ הוּא יָצָא מִמִּצְרָיִם:

B'chol dor vador chayav adam lirot et-atzmo, k'ilu hu yatza mimitzrayim.

In every generation, everyone is obligated to see themselves as though they personally left Egypt.

The Seder reminds us that it was not only our ancestors whom God redeemed; God redeemed us too along with them. That's why the Torah says, "God brought us out from there in order to lead us to and give us the land promised to our ancestors."

The shank bone represents the Lamb Sacrifice made in the days of the Temple for the Passover holiday. It is called the Pesach Lamb, from the Hebrew word meaning "to pass over," because God passed over the houses of our ancestors when visiting plagues upon our oppressors.

The matzah reminds us that when our ancestors were finally free to leave Egypt, there was no time to pack or prepare. Our ancestors grabbed whatever dough was made and set out on their journey, letting their dough bake into matzah as they fled.

The bitter herbs provide a visceral reminder of the bitterness of slavery and the life of forced hard labor our ancestors experienced.

The Seder Plate

Dayenu

We now sing songs praising God to recount the many miracles performed by God for the redemption of the Jewish people.

The plagues and our subsequent redemption are but one example of the care God has given us in our history. Had God but done any one of these kindnesses, it would have been enough – dayenu.

אִלּוּ הוֹצִיאָנוּ מִמִּצְרַיִם, דַּיֵּנוּ:

Ilu hotzi- hotzianu, Hotzianu mi-mitzrayim Hotzianu mi-mitzrayim, Dayenu

If God had only taken us out of Egypt, that would have been enough!

אִלּוּ נָתַן לָנוּ אֶת־הַתּוֹרָה, דַּיֵּנוּ:

Ilu natan natan lanu, natan lanu et ha-Torah, Natan lanu et ha-Torah , Dayenu

If God had only given us the Torah, that would have been enough.

Everyone at the table can sing or recite the following song, Dayenu.

Hebrew Version:	Ilu ho-tsi, ho-tsi-a-nu,
	Ho-tsi-anu mi-Mitz-ra-yim
	Ho-tsi-anu mi-Mitz-ra-yim
	Da-ye-nu
Chorus:	Da-da-ye-nu,
	Da-da-ye-nu,
	Da-da-ye-nu,
	Da-da-ye-nu,
	Da-ye-nu Da-ye-nu

If God had taken us out of Egypt and not executed judgment upon them,
it would've been enough for us–Dayenu.

If God had executed judgment upon them and not upon their idols,
it would've been enough for us–Dayenu.

If God had judged their idols, and not killed their firstborn,
it would've been enough for us–Dayenu.

If God had killed their firstborn, and not given us their wealth,
it would've been enough for us–Dayenu.

If God had given us their wealth, and not split the sea for us,
it would've been enough for us–Dayenu.

If God had split the sea for us, and not let us through it on dry land,
it would've been enough for us–Dayenu.

If God had let us through it on dry land, and not drowned our enemies in it,
it would've been enough for us–Dayenu.

If God had drowned our enemies in it, and not provided for our needs in the desert for 40 years,
it would've been enough for us–Dayenu.

The Ten Plagues

As we rejoice at our deliverance from slavery, we acknowledge our freedom was hard-earned.

Dip a finger into the wine and transfer ten drops of wine to your plate as each of the ten plagues visited on Egypt are recited.

Blood

Frogs

Lice

Beasts

Cattle Disease

Boils

Hail

Locusts

Darkness

Death of the Firstborn

God chose Moses to lead the Jews out of slavery to freedom. Moses encountered God at the burning bush and returned to Egypt to lead us out of slavery. He demanded that Pharaoh let the Jewish people go.

Sing or say the words to "Go Down Moses."

When Israel was in Egypt's land,
Let my people go;
Oppressed so hard they could not stand,
Let my people go.

Chorus:
Go down, Moses,
Way down in Egypt's land;
Tell old Pharaoh
To let my people go!

"Thus saith the Lord," bold Moses said,
Let my people go;
"If not, I'll smite your first-born dead,"
Let my people go.

Chorus

No more shall they in bondage toil,
Let my people go;
Let them come out with Egypt's spoil,
Let my people go.

Chorus

The Four Children

We are told of four different types of children who might react differently to the Passover Seder. It is our job to make our story accessible to all the members of our community.

The wise child asks, "What are the testimonies and laws that God commanded you?"

You must teach this child the rules of observing the holiday of Passover.

The wicked child asks, "What does this service mean to you?"

To you and not to himself! Because he takes himself out of the community and misses the point, set this child's teeth on edge and say to him, "It is because of what God did for me in taking me out of Egypt." Me, not him. Had that child been there, he would have been left behind.

The simple child asks, "What is this?"

To this child, answer plainly. "With a strong hand God took us out of Egypt, where we were slaves."

What about the child who doesn't know how to ask a question?

Help this child to ask. Start telling the story. "It is because of what God did for me in taking me out of Egypt."

שֶׁבְּכָל הַלֵּילוֹת אָנוּ אוֹכְלִין חָמֵץ וּמַצָּה. הַלַּיְלָה הַזֶּה כֻּלּוֹ מַצָּה:

She-bichol ha-lei-lot anu och'lin cha-meitz u-matzah. Ha-lai-la ha-zeh kulo matzah.

**On all other nights we eat both leavened bread and matzah.
Tonight we only eat matzah.**

שֶׁבְּכָל הַלֵּילוֹת אָנוּ אוֹכְלִין בֵּין יוֹשְׁבִין וּבֵין מְסֻבִּין. הַלַּיְלָה הַזֶּה כֻּלָּנוּ מְסֻבִּין:

She-bichol ha-lei-lot ain anu mat-bilin afi-lu pa-am echat. Ha-lai-la ha-zeh shtei fi-amim.

**On all other nights we aren't expected to dip our vegetables one time.
Tonight we do it twice.**

שֶׁבְּכָל הַלֵּילוֹת אָנוּ אוֹכְלִין שְׁאָר יְרָקוֹת הַלַּיְלָה הַזֶּה מָרוֹר:

She-bichol ha-leilot a-nu ochlin shi'ar yirakot ha-leila ha-zeh maror.

On all other nights we eat all kinds of vegetables, but tonight we eat bitter herbs.

שֶׁבְּכָל הַלֵּילוֹת אָנוּ אוֹכְלִין בֵּין יוֹשְׁבִין וּבֵין מְסֻבִּין. הַלַּיְלָה הַזֶּה כֻּלָּנוּ מְסֻבִּין:

She-bichol ha-leilot a-nu ochlin bein yoshvin uvein m'subin. Ha-laila h-azeh ku-lanu m'subin.

On all other nights we eat either sitting normally or reclining. Tonight we recline.

> The rest of the Maggid answers the question with the story of the Hebrews' Exodus from Egypt, some Torah study, and a discussion of the description of the four types of children; the wise child, the wicked child, the simple child, and the child who doesn't know enough to ask a question.

עֲבָדִים הָיִינוּ הָיִינוּ. עַתָּה בְּנֵי חוֹרִין:

Avadim hayinu hayinu. Ata b'nei chorin.

We were slaves. Now we are free.

Everyone recites the answer:

We were slaves to Pharaoh, and God took us from there with a strong hand and outstretched arm. Had God not brought our ancestors out of captivity, then even today we and our children and our grandchildren would still be slaves. Even if we were all wise, knowledgeable scholars and Torah experts, we would still be obligated to tell the story of the Exodus.

Raise the glass of wine and say:

וְהִיא שֶׁעָמְדָה לַאֲבוֹתֵינוּ וְלָנוּ.

V'hi she-amda l'a-vo-teinu v'lanu.

This promise has sustained our ancestors and us.

For not only one enemy has risen against us to annihilate us, but in every generation there are those who rise against us. But God saves us from those who seek to harm us.

Put the glass of wine down.

In the years our ancestors lived in Egypt, our numbers grew, and soon the family of Jacob became the People of Israel. Pharaoh, alarmed by this growing great nation, enslaved us. He forced us to perform hard labor. Fearing that even as slaves we would grow stronger and rebel, Pharaoh decreed that Israelite baby boys should be drowned to prevent the Israelites from overthrowing those who had enslaved them.

While traditionally the youngest child now asks the Four Questions, any person, or everyone together, can read them.

The four questions all ask the same thing in different ways.

מַה נִּשְׁתַּנָּה הַלַּיְלָה הַזֶּה מִכָּל הַלֵּילוֹת?

Ma nish-tana ha-lai-la ha-zeh mi-kol ha-lei-lot?

Why is this night different from all other nights?

Step 5: Maggid—Our Story

Take the Seder plate off the table, pour a second cup of wine (but don't drink it!), and recite the story of Exodus.

Our story starts in ancient times when Abraham decided to stop worshiping idols. The idea of one God, invisible and all-powerful, inspired him to start a new community in Canaan, the land that would one day become Israel.

God promised Abraham that his family would become a great nation, but this promise came with a caveat. There would be trouble as well: "Your descendants will dwell for a time in a land that is not their own, and they will be enslaved and afflicted for four hundred years; but I will punish the nation that enslaved them, and afterwards they shall leave with great wealth."

Step 4: Yachatz—Breaking the Matzah

We eat matzah in memory of the quick flight of our ancestors from captivity in Egypt. As slaves, they suffered greatly before being let go. When they got the chance to be free, they took whatever dough they had and ran, fearing that Pharoah might change his mind again. Baking the unrisen dough resulted in something that looked like the matzah of today.

Uncover and hold up the three matzahs and say:

> This is the bread of poverty that our ancestors ate in the land of Egypt. All who are hungry, come and eat; all who are needy, come and celebrate Passover with us. This year we are here; next year we will be in Israel. This year we are slaves; next year we will be free.

Break the middle matzah on the Seder plate in two. Wrap the larger part in a napkin and put it aside for later use as the afikoman. The smaller piece is put back in between the other two pieces of matzah.

This recalls God's splitting of the Red Sea allowing us to cross onto dry land. The broken middle matzah symbolizes humility, and will be eaten later as the "bread of poverty."

In some families, the afikomen is taken away and hidden somewhere in the house for the children to search for towards the end of the meal.

Another common practice is to place the afikomen near the leader. The kids must steal it during the Seder without the leader noticing.

In some Sephardic families, each person places a broken afikomen matzah on his or her shoulder, symbolizing the quick Exodus from Egypt.

Step 3: Karpas—the "Appetizer"

Passover combines the celebration of an event from our past with recognition of the cycles of nature. As we remember our ancestors' liberation, we also see the stirrings of spring and rebirth around us. The symbols on our table combine elements of both.

Bo-ruch a-toh Ado-noi E-lo-hei-nu
me-lech ho-olom, borei p'ree ha-adama.

We praise God, Ruler of Everything,
who creates the fruits of the earth.

The green vegetable is a symbol of spring and renewal.

The saltwater represents the tears of our ancestors in Egypt. Dipping the karpas in saltwater arouses our curiosity.

Dip a small piece of parsley into saltwater and eat it after reciting the blessing over vegetables.

Step 2: Urchatz—Purification

The second step signifies a spiritual cleansing by pouring water over the hands.

> The Seder leader may act as proxy, performing the Urchatz for everyone in attendance.

Wash hands without the customary blessing.

> According to Jewish law, when dipping food into water, the food must be eaten with a utensil or one's hands must be purified by washing.
>
> Now is a good time to take a moment to reflect on what it is that we are about to do.

Why We Recline
In Pharoah's time, only free people had the luxury of reclining while eating. We lean on our left side when drinking the four cups of wine and eating the matzah to accentuate the fact that we are free.

Step 1: Kadesh—the Benediction

The Seder service begins by proclaiming the holiness of the holiday.

Lift up your cup (traditionally filled by someone else) in your right hand and recite the following:

בָּרוּךְ אַתָּה יְיָ, אֱלֹהֵינוּ מֶלֶךְ הָעוֹלָם, בּוֹרֵא פְּרִי הַגָּפֶן:

Bo-ruch a-toh Ado-noi E-lo-hei-nu me-lech ho-olom, borei p'ree haga-fen.

We praise God, Ruler of Everything, who creates the fruit of the vine.

> *Add in the text in parentheses below if your Seder falls on Friday night.*

We praise God, Ruler of Everything, who gave us a heritage that endures through the ages, ever changing and ever meaningful. We thank You for the opportunities for holiness, the obligations of Your commandments, and the happiness of (Shabbat and) joyful holidays. Together we celebrate (Shabbat and) the Holiday of Matzah, the time of liberation, by reading our sacred stories, remembering the Exodus, and raising our voices in song. We praise God, who sanctifies the family of Israel, (Shabbat) and the holidays.

We praise God, Ruler of Everything, who has kept us alive, raised us up, and brought us to this happy moment.

> *If your Seder falls on a Saturday night, add:*
>
> **Praised are You, Ruler of Everything, who creates the lights of fire.**

Drink the first cup of wine while leaning to the left.

> Wine symbolizes liberation and joy.

Let the Seder Begin

Light the Candles

בָּרוּךְ אַתָּה יי אֱלֹהֵינוּ מֶלֶךְ הָעוֹלָם, אֲשֶׁר קִדְּשָׁנוּ בְּמִצְוֹתָיו וְצִוָּנוּ לְהַדְלִיק נֵר שֶׁל יוֹם טוֹב.

Bo-ruch a-toh Ado-noi E-lo-hei-nu me-lech ho-olom a-sher ki-de-sha-nu be-mitz-vo-sov ve-tzi-vo-nu le-had-lik ner shel Yom Tov.

Blessed are You, Lord our God, Ruler of Everything, who makes us holy with commandments and commands us to light the festival lights.

If Passover falls on a Friday night, use the following prayer:

Bo-ruch a-toh Ado-noi E-lo-hei-nu me-lech ho-olom a-sher ki-de-sha-nu be-mitz-vo-sov ve-tzi-vo-nu le-had-lik ner shel Sha-bos v'shel Yom Tov.

Blessed are you, Lord our God, Ruler of Everything, who has sanctified us with commandments, and has commanded us to kindle the light of the Sabbath and the Festival Day.

Bo-ruch a-toh Ado-noi E-lo-hei-nu me-lech ho-olom, she-he-che-ya-nu vi-kee-yi-ma-nu vi-hi-gee-an-u liz-man ha-zeh.

Blessed are You, Lord our God, Ruler of Everything, who has kept us alive, sustained us and enabled us to celebrate this joyous occasion.

Why Are We Here?

We are here to perform the Seder. We will recount the descent of our Patriarchs; Abraham, Isaac and Jacob into Egypt with the Jewish People. We will recall their suffering and persecution. We will be with them as God sends the Ten Plagues to punish Pharaoh and his nation, and follow along as our Patriarchs leave Egypt and cross the Red Sea. We will witness the miraculous hand of God parting the waters to allow the Israelites to pass.

The basic text we will use, the Haggadah, is almost identical to that used in the eleventh century. We are performing the same ceremony and rituals that our ancestors have for centuries and that Jews all over the world are performing tonight.

This Haggadah is a book of instructions, prayers, blessings, and stories. It lays out the proper order for the Passover Seder. Haggadah means "the telling." The recitation, or telling, of the Exodus story is in fact one of the most important aspects of the Seder.

Prepare the Seder Plate

Set the table with the following:

Zeroa: a roasted bone to bring to mind the original Pesach offering of a lamb.

Charoset: a mixture of nuts, fruit, wine, and spices to bring to mind the mortar our ancestors used to build the pyramids of Egypt.

Maror: bitter herbs, red or white horseradish, to bring to mind the bitterness of Egyptian bondage.

Karpas: usually parsley, to bring to mind hope and renewal.

Beitzah: hard boiled egg, to bring to mind the festival offering in the Temple and the circle of life.

Chazeret: the bitter herb for the "sandwich" that we eat later, following the custom established by Hillel the elder, as a reminder that our ancestors "ate matzah and bitter herbs together." Usually, this piece of horseradish is left in small pieces rather than grated.

A covered plate that holds three pieces of matzah placed at the head of the table.

A bowl of salt water to dip the Karpas.

Wine glasses--one for each person.

An extra wine glass for Elijah the Prophet.

A bowl and pitcher of warm water for the ritual handwashing placed at the head of the table.

The Seder meal should be prepared and conducted without bread or other leavened food.

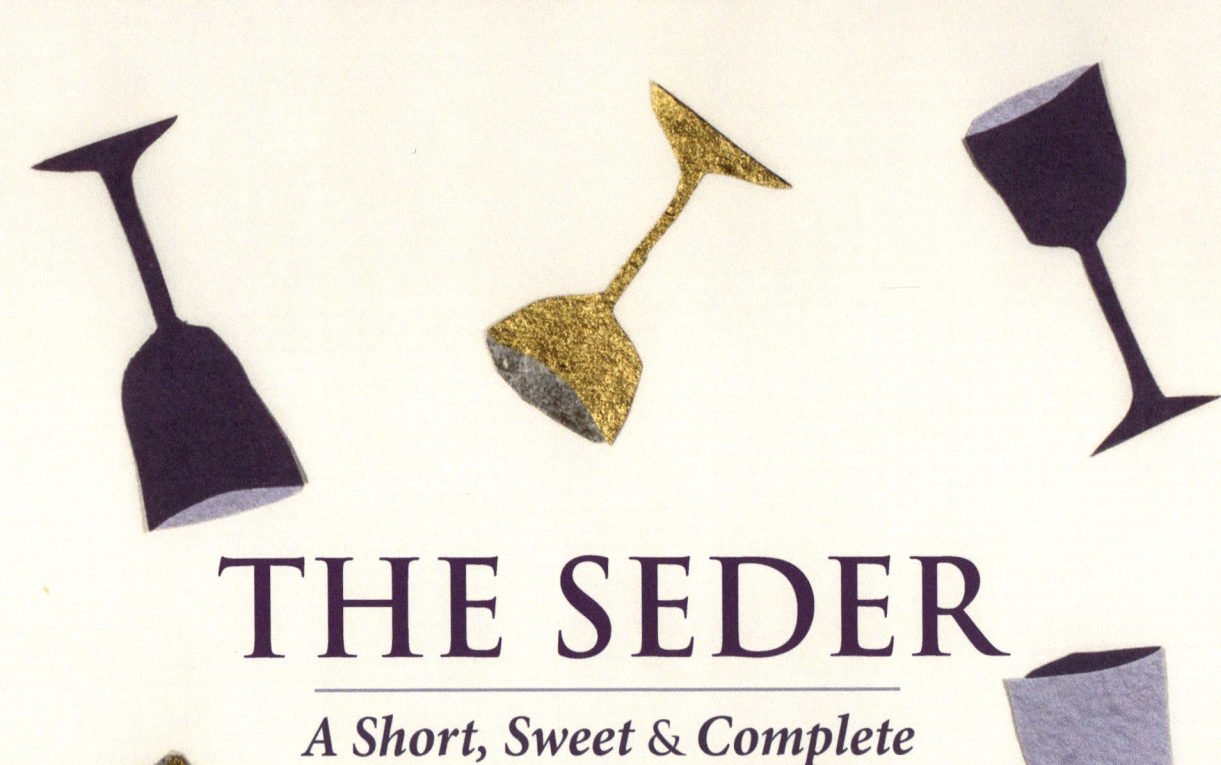

THE SEDER

A Short, Sweet & Complete Passover Haggadah

Edited by Liz Kaplan

Illustrations by
Laura Stillman Carraro

CPSIA information can be obtained
at www.ICGtesting.com
Printed in the USA
BVHW021152250221
601122BV00006B/11